3A
BRAIN ACADEMY
Science

MISSION
FILE 5

John Stringer and
Richard Cooper

Consultant for
NACE: Sue Mordecai

nace

RISING ★ STARS

Rising Stars is grateful to the following people
for their support in developing this series:
Sue Mordecai, Julie Fitzpatrick, Johanna Raffan and Belle Wallace.

NACE, PO Box 242, Arnolds Way, Oxford OX2 9FR
www.nace.co.uk

Rising Stars UK Ltd, 22 Grafton Street, London W1S 4EX
www.risingstars-uk.com

Every effort has been made to trace copyright holders and obtain their permission for
the use of copyright materials. The authors and publisher will gladly receive information
enabling them to rectify any error or omission in subsequent editions.

All facts are correct at time of going to press.

Published 2006
Text, design and layout © Rising Stars UK Ltd.

Editorial Consultant: Sue Mordecai
Technical Consultant: Helen Wilson
Design: Hart McLeod
Illustrations: Cover – Burville-Riley / Characters – Bill Greenhead
Cover Design: Burville-Riley

British Library Cataloguing in Publication Data.
A CIP record for this book is available from the British Library.

ISBN: 978-1-84680-030-6

Printed by Craft Print, Singapore

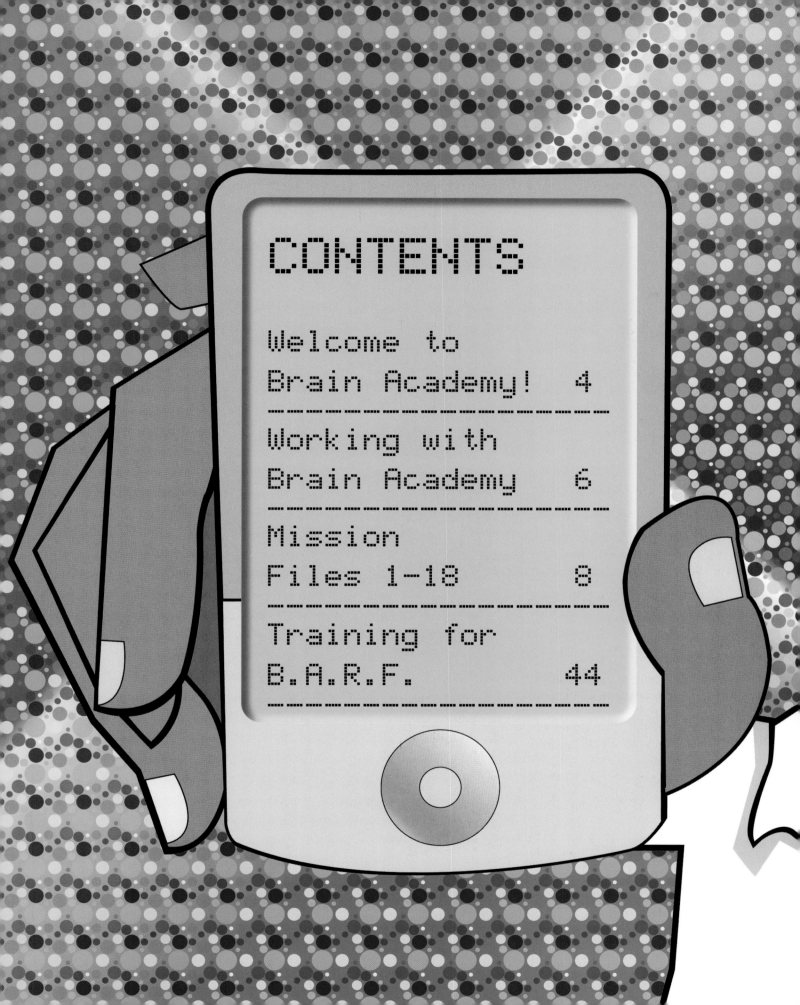

CONTENTS

Welcome to Brain Academy!

Welcome to Brain Academy! Make yourself at home. We are here to give you the low-down on the organisation — so pay attention!

It's our job to help Da Vinci and his colleagues to solve the tough problems they face and we would like you to join us as members of the Academy. Are you up to the challenge?

Da Vinci
Da Vinci is the founder and head of the Brain Academy. He is all seeing, all thinking and all knowing — possibly the cleverest person alive. Nobody has ever actually seen him in the flesh as he communicates only via computer. When Da Vinci receives an emergency call for help, the members of Brain Academy jump into action (and that means you!).

Huxley
Huxley is Da Vinci's right-hand man. Not as clever, but still very smart. He is here to guide you through the missions and offer help and advice. The sensible and reliable face of Brain Academy, Huxley is cool under pressure.

Dr Hood
The mad doctor is the arch-enemy of Da Vinci and Brain Academy. He has set up a rival organisation called D.A.F.T. (which stands for Dull And Feeble Thinkers). Dr Hood and his agents will do anything they can to irritate and annoy the good people of this planet. He is a pain we could do without.

Hilary Kumar
Ms Kumar is the Prime Minister of our country. As the national leader she has a hotline through to the Academy but will only call in an extreme emergency. Confident and strong willed, she is a very tough cookie indeed.

General Cods-Wallop
This highly decorated gentleman (with medals, not wallpaper) is in charge of the armed forces. Most of his success has come from the help of Da Vinci and the Academy rather than the use of his somewhat limited military brain.

Mrs Tiggles
Stella Tiggles is the retired head of the Secret Intelligence service. She is a particular favourite of Da Vinci who treats her as his own mother. Mrs Tiggles' faithful companion is her cat, Bond... James Bond.

We were just like you once — ordinary schoolchildren leading ordinary lives. Then one day we all received a call from a strange character named Da Vinci. From that day on, we have led a double life — as secret members of Brain Academy!

Here are a few things you should know about the people you'll meet on your journey.

Echo the Eco-Warrior

Echo is the hippest chick around. Her love of nature and desire for justice will see her do anything to help an environmental cause — even if it means she's going to get her clothes dirty.

Maryland T. Wordsworth

M.T. Wordsworth is the president of the USA. Not the sharpest tool in the box, Maryland prefers to be known by his middle name, Texas, or 'Tex' for short. He takes great exception to being referred to as 'Mary' (which has happened in the past).

Buster Crimes

Buster is a really smooth dude and is in charge of the Police Force. His laid-back but efficient style has won him many friends, although these don't include Dr Hood or the agents of D.A.F.T. who regularly try to trick the coolest cop in town.

Sandy Buckett

The fearless Sandy Buckett is the head of the fire service. Sandy and her team of brave firefighters are always on hand, whether to extinguish the flames of chaos caused by the demented Dr Hood or just to rescue Mrs Tiggles' cat…

Anna Lyse

Da Vinci has recently recruited Anna Lyse to run B.A.R.F. (the Brain Academy Research Facility), where her job is to manage the best scientists to carry out investigations for the advancement of human knowledge. The micro-processor implanted into her brain allows her to be permanently and wirelessly connected to the Internet… but it does have its drawbacks when Victor uses her search engine…

Victor Blastov

Victor Blastov is the leading scientist at the Space Agency. He once tried to build a rocket by himself but failed to get the lid off the glue. Victor often requires the services of the Academy, even if it's to set the video to record Dr Who.

Prince Barrington

Prince Barrington, or 'Bazza' as he is known to his friends, is the publicity-seeking heir to the throne. Always game for a laugh, the Prince will stop at nothing to raise money for worthy causes. Definitely a 'good egg'.

Working with Brain Academy

Do you get the idea? Now you've had the introduction we are going to show you the best way to use this book.

MISSION FILE 5:8

Getting to the 'core' of a great discovery...

The plot

This tells you what the mission is about.

Sir Isaac Newton was one of the greatest scientists of all time.

I agree, sir. Didn't he write the laws of gravity?

Legend has it that the theory came to him whilst sitting under an apple tree. An apple dropped and hit him on the head.

Hmm. Good job he wasn't sitting under a coconut tree!

TM Force is measured in 'Newtons'. Follow these instructions to make a 'force meter'.

1. Knot two strong rubber bands around a 10cm length of PVC plumbing pipe.

2. Screw a cup hook into the end of 30cm of 3cm² wood.

3. Slide the pipe over the wood.

4. Loop the rubber bands round the hook.

5. Mark the wood with a scale by making equally spaced pencil marks and numbering them.

Test it. Hold the tube and use the hook to pull things along. Hold the tube and use the hook to push. Watch the scale.

22

The Training Mission

This short assignment will get you thinking about some key scientific ideas.

Each mission is divided up into different parts.

No one said this was easy. In fact that is why you have been chosen. Da Vinci will only take the best and he believes that includes you. Good luck!

Each book contains a number of 'missions' for you to take part in. The characters in Brain Academy are always on hand to introduce each mission to you.

The Main Mission

This is where you get to do the experiments and complete the challenge.

M1 Use your force meter first to estimate, and then to measure, push and pull forces.

- Try pulling things along.
- Try pushing things.

Collect your data in two columns – one for your estimate, and one for your measurement.

Try picking things up with the meter. This is a special case of 'pull force' – the pull of gravity or 'weight'.

What is the weight of a medium-sized apple like Isaac Newton's?

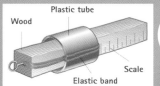

Wood
Plastic tube
Scale
Elastic band

Apple (a) falling at 35mph x gravity (gy)/80g x 25 feet = Large bump on head!

The Da Vinci Files

These problems are for the best Brain Academy recruits.

Da Vinci files

Gravity shapes our bodies. We are the shape we are because of gravity. We need muscles and bones, shaped as they are, to keep our body shape against the pull of gravity. Find out more about the physical changes to the body during and after space travel.

ANALYSE THIS!

What happens when an irresistible force meets an immovable object?

P3

Analyse This!

Anna's always on the look-out for new B.A.R.F staff... Are you tough enough to take on her recruitment challenge?

PS: See pages 46–47 for a useful thinking process!

Garden gourmet!

My garden lawn needs feeding. Do you think you could sort that out for me, Victor?

Of course, sir. Vood ze lawn like to see a menu?

Hmm... I think I'll call Echo instead!

Victor is convinced that you need to feed healthy plants. He thinks cola or milk should be ideal plant food.

Plan and carry out a test using cola, milk and water for watering healthy plants.

Milk and cola are mostly water. Explain your results.

8

I've sent Victor to buy some lawn feed. I hope he knows the difference between the Garden Centre and the Butcher's Shop!

SAFETY: Wear plastic gloves to handle grass seed. Use a throwaway spoon for fertiliser.

Grass grows because green plants make their own food from water and carbon dioxide, using light from the Sun. But plants need tiny amounts of other materials, too. They get these from the soil. Adding fertiliser gives more of these materials.

Plant some grass seed. Compare growing it using fertiliser and water with just water.

Which fertiliser makes grass grow best? Plant some grass seed and find out.

First decide:

• What do you mean by 'best grass'?

• How will you make sure the only thing you change is the fertiliser?

• What did you find was the best fertiliser for grass? How do you know?

Da Vinci files

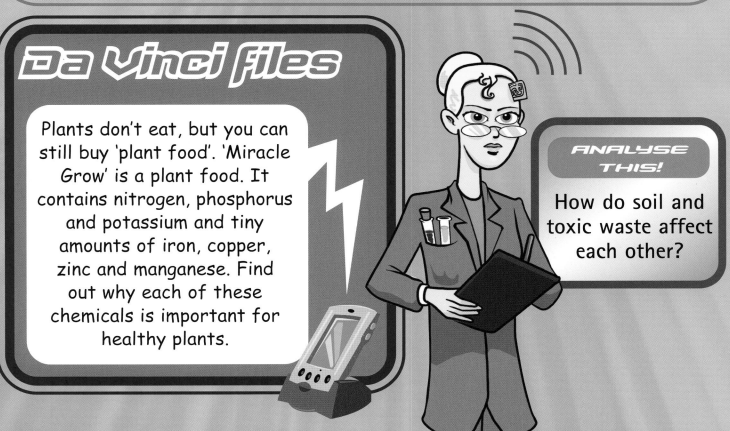

Plants don't eat, but you can still buy 'plant food'. 'Miracle Grow' is a plant food. It contains nitrogen, phosphorus and potassium and tiny amounts of iron, copper, zinc and manganese. Find out why each of these chemicals is important for healthy plants.

ANALYSE THIS!

How do soil and toxic waste affect each other?

P... P... Picture a penguin

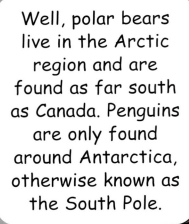

Why don't polar bears eat penguins?

Well, polar bears live in the Arctic region and are found as far south as Canada. Penguins are only found around Antarctica, otherwise known as the South Pole.

I thought it was because they couldn't get the wrappers off with their paws!

Ask a teacher or a friend to find a picture of a named type of penguin, cover its name and give you the picture.

Answer these questions:

1 Does your penguin have a long, thin beak? Go to step 2.

   Does it have a short, thick beak? Go to step 3.

2 Does your penguin have a comma patch on its head? It is a *King penguin*.

   Does it have a patch like a D on its head? It is an *Emperor penguin*.

3 Does your penguin have a completely black head? It is an *Adelie penguin*.

   Does it have light-coloured patches or stripes on its head? Go to step 4.

4 Does your penguin have a tuft of feathers on its head? It is a *Rockhopper penguin*.

   If it does not have a tuft of feathers on its head, go to step 5.

5 Does your penguin have a thin line across its face? It is a *Chinstrap penguin*.

   Does it have a light patch above one eye? It is a *Gentoo penguin*.

M1

Bazza would put all mini-beasts into one category: 'Horrible creepy-crawlies!'

Make your own key like the one above for the penguins. Use pictures of six or eight small invertebrates or minibeasts. Remember to ask questions that can be answered with 'yes' or 'no'.

1 Write your own questions to split your group of minibeasts into two – maybe a question about legs.

2 Now write another question that will split one of the smaller groups into two. You might use questions about where the animals live.

3 Go on asking questions that will split the groups until each minibeast is in a group of its own.

Ask a friend to try your key. Does it work?

Da Vinci files

Use this interactive woodlouse key to identify a woodlouse: www.nhm.ac.uk/woodlice/identification.html

ANALYSE THIS!

Do fish have a sense of smell?

'Mould blend' coffee cup

Vood you like to meet my new pet? Its name is Herbie.

Where is he and what is he?

'It' lives in a coffee cup I found under ze bed. Look, it is a giant mould zat has grown over ze top of ze cup!

Eurgh!

TM We keep foods for longer by drying, canning in 'tins', chilling, freezing, pickling in vinegar, salting and preserving in sugar.

Match each of these foods to the usual way of keeping it:

fish fingers   corned beef   jam   beetroot   butter
instant coffee   baked beans

All these treatments slow, or stop, the growth of micro-organisms like moulds.

So, if these methods slow growth, just what conditions do moulds grow best in?

Herbie 'grows on you' over the years!

Grow some mould on white and brown bread, normal and 'long life', both fresh and toasted. Seal each slice tightly inside a clear plastic sandwich bag and leave all six in a warm place. Check the bread regularly but don't open the bags!

Which grows mould first? Why do you think that is? What conditions help mould grow fast? Do dampness or warmth matter? Why does toasting make a difference? Does long life bread stay fresher, longer? How do you know?

Repeat the investigation with baked bread and bread dough. Which grows mould first? Knowing what you do about mould, can you explain why?

Throw the bags away, UNOPENED!

Da Vinci files

It's easy to make a magnifier with a water drop. Make a tiny hole in a strip of cardboard with a sharp pencil, being careful not to push the point into your hand. Stick clear tape over the hole. Using the pencil point, put a drop of water on the tape over the hole. Hold the water drop over a page of print and see how the letters are enlarged. Look at the gills of a mushroom with your magnifier.

ANALYSE THIS!

Do all foods go bad?

13

Yummy yoghurts

Arggh! I've just eaten one of Bazza's hot chilli prawn kebabs!

Will you never learn? He's about as much use in the kitchen as a plastic tea-towel!

I've drunk ten litres of water and my mouth still hurts.

Eat this tub of yoghurt. That should cool it down.

TM Make some yoghurt. Everything you use must be perfectly clean and an adult *must* do the boiling. The temperature needs to be exactly right.

1 Boil a pint of fresh pasteurised milk. Simmer it gently for thirty minutes until the milk has lost a third of its water.

2 Tip the milk into a clean jug, and cool it to 49°C.

3 Put half a teaspoon of any natural unsweetened yoghurt – the starter – into a thermos flask. Add a little milk, stir well, and add the rest of the milk.

4 Put the lid on, and leave it for six hours or more.

5 At the end of this time you should have three-quarters of a pint of natural yoghurt. You can store it in the refrigerator.

The starter yoghurt contains living micro-organisms. Why do you think they multiply in the fresh, warm milk?

M1 You can make this soft cheese very quickly, and eat it at once. Everything you use must be perfectly clean and you *must* ask an adult to help you with the heating.

1. Squeeze the juice from a large lemon. Put it in a large bowl.

2. Heat one pint of pasteurised milk in a saucepan to exactly 38°C. Remove it from the heat.

3. Pour the warmed milk on to the lemon juice and stir gently. It will separate into 'curds' (solid matter) and 'whey' (liquid).

4. Line a sieve with a clean J–cloth and place it over a saucepan or bowl.

5. Pour or spoon the curds into the sieve.

6. Gather the corners of the cloth together, and tie them with a piece of string.

7. Hang the cheese over the bowl to drain for ten minutes.

8. Put the cheese on a plate and add salt. Eat it immediately, or wrap and refrigerate it.

Da Vinci files

Find the answers to these questions from the Internet — and from yoghurt pots!

1 How was yoghurt first made?
2 What colours and preservatives are there in packaged yoghurt?
3 Why keep yoghurt in the refrigerator?

ANALYSE THIS!

Which food would make the best glue?

Sweet old Mrs T!

> Oooo, I do like a nice piece of cake with my tea.

> Which is your favourite? Sponge, creamy ones, fruit or cup-cakes, maybe?

> Why don't you take me out to tea and we'll find out!

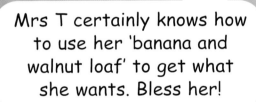

> Mrs T certainly knows how to use her 'banana and walnut loaf' to get what she wants. Bless her!

TM

Mrs Tiggles likes sugar in her tea – lots of sugar.

What do you think happens if you keep adding sugar to tea – or to water?

What will happen to the tea level with:

- a little sugar?

- some more sugar?

- lots of sugar?

Why?

Why does the surface of tea go down when you first add sugar? It has to do with the spaces between particles...

M1

Nice of me to invite the local OAP group as well. Da Vinci's screen was flashing red he was so pleased!

A see-saw balance is holding two containers of water which weigh the same – one is pure water, the other is salt water. At first, the containers balance. Then the sun comes up.

Predict what will happen as the water evaporates. Remember that:

- salt dissolves in water

- water evaporates

- when salt water evaporates, salt is left behind.

Salt does not evaporate at low temperatures.

Draw what you think will happen as the water evaporates – and why. Then try it.

Da Vinci files

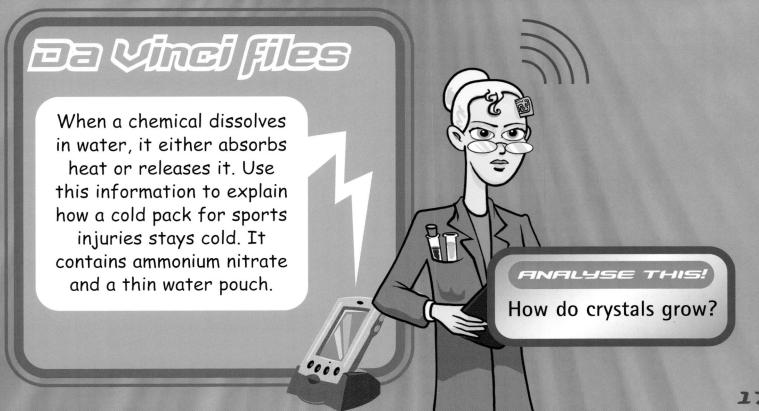

When a chemical dissolves in water, it either absorbs heat or releases it. Use this information to explain how a cold pack for sports injuries stays cold. It contains ammonium nitrate and a thin water pouch.

ANALYSE THIS!

How do crystals grow?

Get a handle on these candles!

If I get another scented candle for my birthday I will crash, I know I will.

Calm down sir, scented candles are meant to have a soothing effect on one's mood.

They might soothe me if I could light one. I can't even open the box of matches!

A wax candle is fuel. Fuels are a source of energy. Try this task together with an adult. Fix a candle safely upright. Light it with a match. Draw the top of the candle and the flame. On your drawing of the candle label the following parts:

the solid wax   the liquid wax   the unburnt wax gas
the burning wax gas   the soot

If you carefully hold a jar or tin of ice in the top of the candle flame, soot will collect on it. You will also see drops of a colourless liquid condense on it.

- What is the liquid?

- Where has it come from?

An invisible gas has been produced, too.

- What is it?

- Where has it come from?

M1

Candles need fuel and air to burn. They will not burn in very cold conditions. Put the candle out, several times over, in different ways. Explain why the candle is going out.

- Why does it go out when you blow?
- Why does it go out if you snuff it?
- Why might it go out in a freezer?

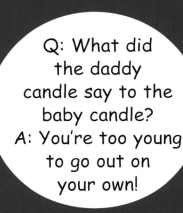

Q: What did the daddy candle say to the baby candle?
A: You're too young to go out on your own!

Da Vinci files

Candle wicks have a natural curl. But they are stretched out straight and held straight by the candle wax inside the candle. Where they come out of the top of the candle they curl over. Look carefully at a burning candle. Why don't you need to 'trim the wick' — that is, cut the candle wick — as it grows longer and longer?

ANALYSE THIS!

Do scented candles burn slower or faster? Why?

A home-made chemistry set

My experiment has gone wrong. I've just blown up my lab!

Good grief, what happened? Are you okay?

Ja. Luckily Sandy turned up to put ze fire out.

What were you experimenting on?

I vos trying to see if the fireworks in ze old box I found still worked. And zey did!

Time to do some mixing!

SAFETY: These are kitchen chemicals, but even kitchen chemicals can be harmful if mixed wrongly. And some chemicals – like bleach – are dangerous, anyway.

Try mixing small quantities of:

- vinegar and bicarbonate of soda
- water with Plaster of Paris
- lemon juice and washing soda
- water to cornflour, stirring as you add it.

Also try mixing cement powder and water (but make sure you wear gloves to do this).

After mixing these substances then observe and record any changes in temperature, hardness and bubbling.

Old fireworks, gunpowder and matches. Add one fool, and stand vell back!

Time for the Mystery of the White Powders... Prepare a kitchen quiz for your friends.

Put a spoonful of each of the following into separate yoghurt pots: flour, icing sugar, table salt, rock salt, cornflour, self-raising flour, white washing powder and bicarbonate of soda. Label them with a secret code.

- Ask your friends to try to identify them through their appearance, smell and touch – but not their taste! (Tell them to be careful when sniffing not to breathe in the smell too much.)

- Ask them to add water or vinegar to each of the samples.

- Ask them to identify – name – each of the white powders.

Da Vinci files

Make your own plastic. Add borax crystals to warm water, stirring until the water will take no more. Add it, a little at a time, to PVA adhesive – white glue. Keep stirring as the glue absorbs the borax. The PVA will become rubbery and can be shaped. It will dry out hard over several days, keeping its shape. Paint or varnish it.

ANALYSE THIS!

What is the best solution for blowing bubbles?

Getting to the 'core' of a great discovery...

Sir Isaac Newton was one of the greatest scientists of all time.

I agree, sir. Didn't he write the laws of gravity?

Legend has it that the theory came to him whilst sitting under an apple tree. An apple dropped and hit him on the head.

Hmm. Good job he wasn't sitting under a coconut tree!

TM Force is measured in 'Newtons'. Follow these instructions to make a 'force meter'.

1 Knot two strong rubber bands around a 10cm length of PVC plumbing pipe.

2 Screw a cup hook into the end of 30cm of $3cm^2$ wood.

3 Slide the pipe over the wood.

4 Loop the rubber bands round the hook.

5 Mark the wood with a scale by making equally spaced pencil marks and numbering them.

Test it. Hold the tube and use the hook to pull things along. Hold the tube and use the hook to push. Watch the scale.

Use your force meter first to estimate, and then to measure, push and pull forces.

- Try pulling things along.
- Try pushing things.

Collect your data in two columns – one for your estimate, and one for your measurement.

Try picking things up with the meter. This is a special case of 'pull force' – the pull of gravity or 'weight'.

What is the weight of a medium-sized apple like Isaac Newton's?

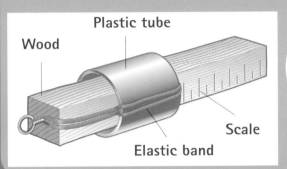

Wood
Plastic tube
Scale
Elastic band

Apple (a) falling at 35mph x gravity (gy)/80g x 25 feet = Large bump on head!

Da Vinci files

Gravity shapes our bodies. We are the shape we are because of gravity. We need muscles and bones, shaped as they are, to keep our body shape against the pull of gravity. Find out more about the physical changes to the body during and after space travel.

ANALYSE THIS!

What happens when an irresistible force meets an immovable object?

Buster is 'floating and gloating'!

Our new police boats are the coolest on the waves!

My new fire boat has got all the latest fire-fighting technology.

Sure, but I bet it doesn't have 2 x 10 Subwoofers AW1000N and 2 x A1504DP amplifiers mounted in the black leather trim cabin!

TM

Put a large lump of Plasticine in water. It sinks.

Now try to shape it so that it floats.

One trick is to roll it out flat with a pastry roller. Bend up the edges and make a hollow boat.

Give two reasons why it might float. Think about what it contains. Think about what happens to the water when you take the boat out!

Why did the boat float, when the lump sank?

How much load will the boat carry before it sinks?

M1

You won't catch me in no Plasticine boat, dude!

Hang your lump of Plasticine from a Newton meter or spring balance. Record its weight – the pull downwards due to gravity.

Lower the Plasticine into the water. Record how its weight seems to change.

- What is the reading on the Newton meter when it is partly in the water?
- Then when it is hanging in mid-water?
- Finally, when it is resting on the bottom!

Shape the Plasticine into a boat. Hang this from the meter and try the same test. What is the reading on the Newton meter when it is floating?

Can you think why the readings are changing?

Da Vinci files

Use recycled materials to build an unsinkable boat. It must carry a heavy load and not sink.

ANALYSE THIS!

Why does gravity pull and not push?

Something for Tex to reflect on...

Mirror, mirror on the wall, who's the smartest of them all?

Well, I would nominate Da Vinci, of course.

Not little ol' me?

Sorry Tex, can you lend me your head? I'm building an idiot!

TM

Tape two plastic mirrors together along the edges so that they open and close like a book. Stand them up on the table and put a small object, like an eraser, in the 'V'. Slowly open and close the mirror 'book' and count how many erasers you can see in the mirrors. When can you see three or more?

You could use a protractor to measure the angle between the mirrors. How are the angle and the number of images related?

M1

I guess that told me. I'm not as dumb as I look, you know!

Do this in a shady room.

Tape a piece of card with a slot cut in it over the front of a strong torch resting flat on the table.

Push small plastic mirrors on to lumps of Plasticine, so that they stand up like doors.

Reflect the thin beam of light from the torch by standing a mirror in front of it. Watch how the beam changes direction as you move the mirror.

Now put out several mirror doors on the table and arrange them to play 'light billiards'. The light beam must bounce off each of them until it hits a target.

Draw your winning set-up.

Da Vinci files

Reflection explains why the sky is blue! Add one teaspoon of milk to a straight-sided glass of water and stir. In a dark room, hold a torch above the surface of the water and observe the water in the glass from the side. It should have a slight bluish tint.

Particles of milk in the glass have reflected the light and scattered it as different colours. Blue light is reflected to the side — but you will see a different tint if you look up into the water, or through the water at the torch.

ANALYSE THIS!

Is air absolutely transparent at any distance?

It's just an illusion...

Did you see that magician? He sawed a woman in half!

He didn't really. It was just a trick, an illusion.

Then how did he do it?

Magicians never give their secrets away.

Well, someone must have shown him how to do it or there would have been a few messy practice tries!

Twist the end of a long strip of paper through 180° and glue the ends together to make a ring.

Try colouring the inside and outside different colours.

Try running a felt pen along one edge and see what happens.

This is called a Möbius strip. It is an illusion – a trick. The painter M. C. Escher used illusions like these in his pictures to trick our eyes.

You can make more complex puzzles by twisting the paper through other turns and gluing – a half turn, a whole turn, a turn and a half and so on.

Cut down the centre of each strip and see what you get.

M1

I'm going to take up magic. Now, Echo, have you seen my set of saws and swords? Echo, where are you?

Let's draw a picture with 'depth', in order to create an 'optical illusion'.

Take a piece of paper and draw a horizontal line across the middle of it. This is the imaginary skyline – the horizon.

Put a dot in the middle of the line. This is the vanishing point (VP). Now use your ruler to draw two lines at the bottom of the picture, meeting at the VP. This gives you a road. Draw two lines at the top of the picture, also meeting at the VP.

Between that line and the road, draw in some lamp-posts or some telegraph poles. Remember that they are upright, and must stay upright as they get smaller in the distance!

Now do the same thing in order to put:

- houses on the other side of the road

- people on the road

- trees in the background.

See how you are adding the illusion of depth?

Da Vinci files

Different shapes have different numbers of sides or 'faces', like the Möbius strip. Research the five regular 'Platonic solids'. What mathematical relations can you see between their faces, corners and edges?

ANALYSE THIS!

Do colours affect vision?

Lights out for Da Vinci

Prince Bazza has decorated Barrington Hall with a vast collection of Christmas lights, inflatable reindeers and Santas. It's a real fire hazard!

Looks dreadful as well. And what about all the electricity he's using?

I thought you wouldn't mind if I used your battery and re-charger...

You can't do th... zzzzz!

Make up some Christmas tree lights for a (very!) small tree. Can you make them so that they are all bright? If one goes out, do they all go out?

Draw Rudolph the Reindeer on card. Use a simple circuit with a battery and bulb to light up Rudolph's nose. Put the bulb holder behind the cardboard head, and screw the bulb in from the front, wedging it in the hole. Add an 'on and off' switch, or use a flashing bulb.

Put headlights on a card sleigh, and get them to light up. A simple series circuit will light them. A parallel circuit, where each bulb has its own circuit, will make them brighter.

M1 Imagine that Barrington Hall has two floors and the Prince has a light on the upstairs landing. He wants to be able to switch it on – and off – from both the upstairs landing and the downstairs front hall.

You will need one battery, one light and two switches – one for each floor. Wire these together so that the light can be controlled from the landing or from the front hall. If you find that tough, try two-way switches. These have three terminals – one 'in' and two 'out'. Do they solve the problem?

Draw your solution and explain how it works.

> Don't worry, I'll plug DV back in after Christmas!

Da Vinci files

> Use a shoebox as a room — or as a house. Fix low voltage electrical appliances in it — all from the same battery. Fit lights, a ceiling fan, a doorbell. Fit switches, too!

If you had £1 million to spend on scientific research, what would you spend it on?

Resistance is useful!

My presidential office is a bit too bright. The lighting system is terrible.

Why not adjust the lights by installing dimmer switches?

'Dimmer' switches? I need all my switches to be clever, like me!

TM

Some wires resist the flow of electricity more than others. One such is 'nichrome wire'.

You'll need a metre of this resistance wire.

Make up an 'open' circuit with a bulb and battery and two loose leads. Touching the leads together completes the circuit. The bulb lights.

Connect one lead to your length of resistance wire. Slide the other lead up and down the wire. What happens to the brightness of the bulb?

Explain what you think is happening.

A metre of resistance wire is difficult to handle. Make it into a switch.

Cut a piece of card about 15cm long and 5cm wide. Cut 'teeth' into the long edges with pinking shears. Now wind the resistance wire round the card so that it fits in the teeth, like a flat spring. Tape the ends of the wire down.

Now you have a dimmer switch. Use your open circuit to test it. Attach one lead to the end of the resistance wire. Slide the other lead up and down the 'spring'. What happens to the bulb? Why mustn't the coils of wire touch?

Poor old Tex. Not the brightest bulb in the box, but he means well!

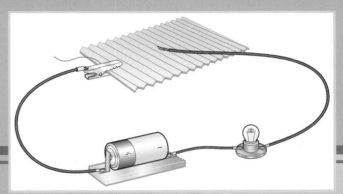

Da Vinci files

Different components have different resistances. Find out what happens with bulbs, buzzers and motors in the same circuit. Record and explain your discoveries.

ANALYSE THIS!

Do all magnets eventually lose their strength?

Dandelion delights!

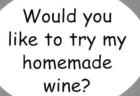

Would you like to try my homemade wine?

Oh yes, thank you. What is it made from?

Dandelions! 'Château de Tiggles'.

(Urgh!) Oh delicious, Mrs T. I prefer your lemonade though!

 Look on a school or sports field, in a garden or a park. Find two dandelions. Find one that is growing out near the middle of the field. Find another that is growing near the border – by a hedge or under a tree.

Draw both dandelions.

Next to each picture, list the differences you can see. Why do you think the two plants look so different? What does it have to do with where they live?

Are the dandelions maybe two different species –'field' dandelions and 'border' dandelions? Try this test to find out.

Swap field dandelions and border dandelions. Cut the base off a washed can – leaving no sharp edges – and tread the can in around a dandelion. Take the plant, together with a core of soil, to another round hole. Water your plants in and mark them. Then wait and see what happens. In the meantime, try to predict the changes and answer these questions:

- What do you think will happen? Will the dandelions change?
- What does your evidence prove?
- How do you know?
- How could you improve the enquiry?

Da Vinci files

Here are some children's ideas.
Which make sense to you?

- There are two different kinds of dandelion growing in different places.
- Dandelions in the middle of the field get trodden flat.
- Dandelions in the middle of the field are flat to get more sun.
- It's darker by the hedge. Plants there have to stretch up to get the sun.
- It's damper by the hedge. Dandelions can grow taller and stronger there.
- The dandelions in the middle of the field are lying down to dodge the mower.

ANALYSE THIS!

Does soil or water temperature affect germination?

The D.A.F.T. lollipop job!

That horrible Hood has replaced all the traffic lights with giant lollipops! He's causing havoc in the city.

I'm relying on you to stop him in his tracks before this gets out of hand.

No problem — with a bit of help! We'll soon have that traffic light terror changed for good!

LED stands for Light Emitting Diode. These tiny, plastic devices light up when low-voltage electricity from a battery passes through them.

Unlike torch bulbs, LEDs are polarised so you have to position them correctly in a circuit. They have two 'legs' that are their electrical connections. You can hold each leg with a crocodile clip (it helps to bend the legs a little so the clips don't touch). One leg should be connected to the positive (+) side of the battery and the other leg to the negative (−) side.

Can you create a circuit using an LED? Don't forget to put it in the circuit the right way round! But which way round is right? Here's a clue: it takes a longer line to draw a plus sign!

Use green, yellow and red LEDs to make a 'traffic light' box outside your head teacher's door. A green light could mean 'come in', a yellow light could mean 'wait' and a red light could mean 'not right now!' The switches could be on the box or they could be inside the head's room – you decide!

How many LEDs will you need? How many switches? How many wires? How can you fix your circuits so that you need only ONE battery for it to work?

Maybe you need to draw this before you start...

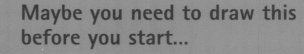

The new traffic lights have saved the day. It's lights out for Dr Hood's sticky scam!

Da Vinci files

Traffic lights go green, then amber (yellow), then red. Then they go red and amber together. Make a working model traffic light with a circuit using three LEDs.

ANALYSE THIS!

How would your life change without electricity?

It's 'snow' joke!

I've been around for so long. My body has changed so much from when I was a young girl.

I wonder what our descendents will look like? Human beings have changed a lot since our first ancestors came down from the trees and walked the Earth.

We won't be around to find out, but I reckon Tex's descendents will be climbing back up the trees!

TM You will need two thermometers and an empty two-litre plastic bottle. Put one thermometer in the bottle and then place the bottle, and the other thermometer, on a windowsill in the Sun. Leave them for a few minutes. What do you notice about each thermometer's temperature? Why do you think this is?

The Earth is surrounded by an invisible layer of gases – just like the bottle around the thermometer. The Sun's heat passes through, reaches the Earth, and is reflected back into space. The layer of gases stops some of this reflection and the thicker the layer, the more heat is kept in. Pollution from the Earth – mostly the waste gas carbon dioxide – is thickening the layer. So more heat is being retained, and the Earth is getting warmer. We call this the 'greenhouse effect' or global warming.

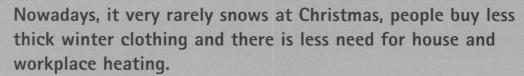

Nowadays, it very rarely snows at Christmas, people buy less thick winter clothing and there is less need for house and workplace heating.

With rising sea levels and less land to live on, perhaps we humans will evolve with webbed feet?!

Ask an older person in your family – a grandparent, for example – to recall what the climate was like when they were a child and record the differences between then and now. Here are some questions to start:

What were winters like when you were a child?

What was the weather like at Christmas/Diwali/other winter festival?

What winter clothes did you wear for school?

How were your journeys affected by the weather?

Tell me about the coldest day you remember.

What garden birds do you remember from winters when you were a child?

When were the first leaves on the trees?

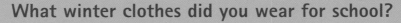

Da Vinci files

The continents are drifting, riding on huge tectonic plates that float on the molten rocks beneath the Earth's surface. In two hundred million years they will have joined together to form a second supercontinent – Pangaea II. Photocopy a map of the world and fit the continents together like a jigsaw to make Pangaea II.

ANALYSE THIS!

If humans became extinct, what species would dominate the planet? Why?

A shirt to dye for!

Hey, Hux, you are one cool customer with that funky shirt!

Errm... Thanks, Buster, but err...

Where did you get it? That new shop in town?

Actually, Buster, it started life as a white shirt but I put it in the wash with my coloureds!

Sweets like Smarties and M&Ms are made brightly coloured by using food dyes. The same dyes can be used in different mixtures to give different colours. How many dyes do you need to colour a tube of different coloured sweets?

SAFETY: If you are diabetic, you mustn't lick or eat the sweets in this task.

You need one sweet of each colour, some absorbent paper and a plastic dropper of clean water. Put the sweets a short distance apart on the paper. Make a note in pencil of the colour of each sweet next to its place on the paper – this is because soon they will all be white! Lick each sweet to remove the 'candy coat', but not the colour. Then drip water – slowly – on to each sweet. Each will leave a coloured smudge. You can see the dyes.

Count each different dye, and then you will know how many dyes are used in the tube.

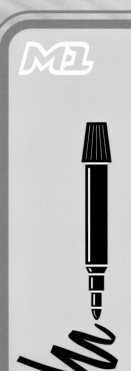

M1
Different pens have different inks in them. Take three different black pens. Make a black mark on a piece of absorbent paper with each pen. (Don't forget to mark the papers so you know which comes from which pen!) Hang each piece in water and watch what happens as the inks 'piggyback' on the rising water.

I could sell shirts like those: 'Buster-Hux' as a brand. I wonder what the logo would look like?

Da Vinci files

Now set your friends a challenge. Take three similar water-soluble pens — all the same colour. Secretly, use one to write a message on a piece of absorbent paper. Give your friends the message and the three pens. Ask them which pen wrote the message.

First, they'll need to write a similar message on absorbent paper with each pen. Then they should hang all the messages so that the end of each paper is in water. The pen can be identified by matching the 'chromatograms' — the blot patterns.

ANALYSE THIS!

Is there any black in the natural world? If yes — where? If no — why?

41

Bazza in bits!

> I have hundreds of pieces of antique porcelain.

> I thought you sold lots of those family heirlooms to raise money for your charities?

> I did, but I've hundreds of pieces of my last vase. I've just knocked it off the mantelpiece. Got any superglue?

TM Solids, liquids and gases are all made up of particles. But some particles are freer to move than others! Copy and complete this table by ticking the boxes in the right places:

Property	Solid	Liquid	Gas
Flows easily and fills containers to give a flat top			
Fills all the space available to it			
Cannot be easily squashed			
Stays the same shape			
Cannot be used to build strong structures			

Filters separate some particles, a bit like a sieve. Instant soup is a good model of mixed particles. Open a packet of instant soup. How would you separate the different 'particles'? Make a plan.

Look at tea bag material or a coffee filter with a hand lens. What can you see? Why is it like this?

Right, I've picked up all 893 pieces. A 3-D jigsaw: what fun!

Da Vinci files

Investigate which liquid moves the fastest. Choose a variety of different liquids, e.g. water, syrup, tomato sauce, vegetable oil, glycerine and cream, and put a measured spoonful of each at the top of a tray. Tip the tray, allowing the liquids to run down it. Which is the fastest? Try timing the liquids. What happens if you cool all the liquids first in a refrigerator? Compare different temperatures of the same liquid. Explain the differences from what you know about particles.

ANALYSE THIS!

How much does the air in your classroom weigh?

Anyone can build a bridge that will stand up. But an engineer can build a bridge that will JUST stand up. In other words, an engineer can build a bridge that does not waste materials. It is strong enough, but not too strong.

Isambard Kingdom Brunel, who was born in 1806, was a great builder of bridges. His famous bridges across the River Tamar at Saltash and across the River Avon in Bristol were amazing feats of engineering and earned him his reputation as the greatest bridge-builder in the Victorian period. He said he built bridges because he was an impatient man, always in a hurry. A bridge cut down the journey time!

His engineering talents didn't stop at bridges. He was chief engineer of the Great Western Railway, overseeing every aspect of railway design, and he was responsible for what was at that time, the largest steamship in the world, The Great Western.

Photographs of him taken at the height of his powers show him wearing the clothes — waistcoat, wing collar, bow tie and tall 'stovepipe' hat — of a wealthy Victorian. But his trousers and boots are dirty... Brunel was always willing to join his workmen in their digging!

Find out more about Brunel and see a photograph of him — at: www.victorianweb.org/technology/engineers/brunel1.html

I looked in ze library and found out that Brunel vos a great engineer from a very young age. He started work on the Thames Tunnel with his father when he vos just 19!

You can build a bridge like Brunel. All you need is the right material – and a gap to cross.

PLANNING
You need some old newspapers and some sticky tape. A real engineer would use as little tape as necessary!

DOING
How good are your bridge-building skills? Tubes are strong. Try rolling up a newspaper. Tape it up. How strong is it? Will it bridge the gap? Maybe not – but a structure built of newspaper tubes might...

REVIEWING
Test your bridge. What is the greatest weight it will take? Careful – don't get your feet in the way, in case it collapses!

YOUR SCIENCE FILE
Photograph your best bridge. Record what you have learned about making a strong, light structure.

You can find out more about Brunel's bridges at these websites:
http://news.bbc.co.uk/1/hi/england/bristol/2968755.stm
www.royal-albert-bridge.co.uk/the_bridge/index.shtml

The TASC Problem Solving Wheel

TASC: Thinking Actively in a Social Context

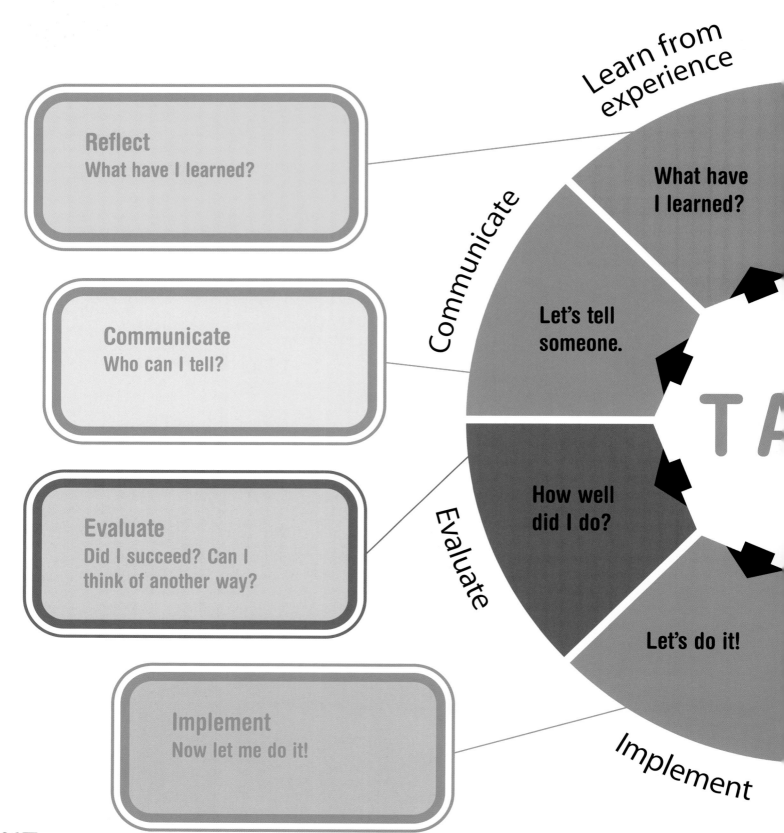

Reflect
What have I learned?

Communicate
Who can I tell?

Evaluate
Did I succeed? Can I
think of another way?

Implement
Now let me do it!

Learn from experience

Communicate

Evaluate

Implement

What have I learned?

Let's tell someone.

How well did I do?

Let's do it!

TA

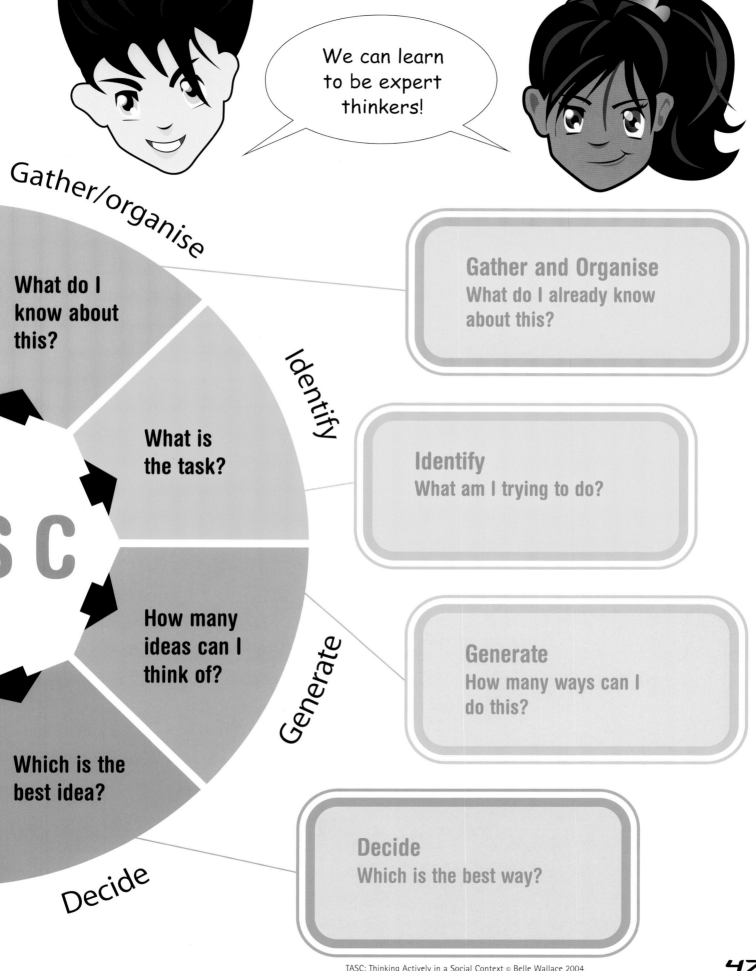

nace

What is NACE?

NACE is a charity which was set up in 1984. It is an organisation that supports the teaching of 'more-able' pupils and helps all children find out what they are good at and to do their best.

What does NACE do?

NACE helps teachers by giving them advice, books, materials and training. Many teachers, headteachers, parents and governors join NACE. Members of NACE can use a special website which gives them useful advice, ideas and materials to help children to learn.

NACE helps thousands of schools and teachers every year. It also helps teachers and children in other countries, such as America and China.

How will this book help me?

Brain Academy Science books challenge and help you to become better at learning by:
• Thinking of and testing different solutions to problems
• Making connections to what you already know
• Making mistakes and learning from them
• Working with your teacher, by yourself and with others
• Expecting you to get better and to go on to the next book
• Learning skills which you can use in other subjects and out of school

We hope that you enjoy the books!

Write to **RISING STARS** and let us know how the books helped you to learn and what you would like to see in the next books.

Rising Stars Ltd, 22 Grafton Street, London W1S 4EX